THE ULTIMATE
REAL ESTATE
MARKETING ASSET

Your Everlasting Marketing Asset That Will Last A Lifetime and How You Can Use It To Attract High-Quality Clients To Achieve Financial Freedom and Build Wealth

11+ Ways Real Estate Professionals Can Use a Book To Gain More High-Quality Clients and Build A Better Real Estate Business

JEROME LEWIS

Published by Jerome Lewis, DRES Media
eBook ISBN: 978-1-960984-15-9
Paperback ISBN: 978-1-960984-13-5
Hardback ISBN: 978-1-960984-14-2

This book is a work of non-fiction. Unless otherwise noted, the author and the publisher make no explicit guarantees as to the accuracy of the information contained in this book and in some cases, names of people and places have been altered to protect their privacy.

Printed in the United States of America.
First Edition: July 2023

Please be advised that the publisher and author of this book are NOT responsible for any errors or omissions in this book. Any legal or financial advice should be evaluated by a professional. The reader of this book is responsible for his or her own due diligence in any business dealings.

For more information, contact Jerome Lewis at Jerome@JeromeLewis.com.

The Ultimate Marketing Asset:

11+ Ways Real Estate Professionals Can Use A Book To Gain More High-Quality Clients And Build A Better Real Estate Business

Free Gift

Download your free gift and companion guide at **REmarketingBook.com/Free**.

Or scan the QR Code Below

Ideas Are Worthless Without Implementation!

Concepts, ideas, and theories… that's the easy stuff. Everybody has ideas. What we need to be looking for is how to apply these ideas. There's no shortage of ideas. But there is definitely a shortage of how to apply, employ, and implement ideas.

If you want **success**, what matters most is **implementation**.

Action, application, execution, and **implementation**. Stop wanting things to be perfect and just **get it done**.

While others hesitate, you **demonstrate**.

- **Speed** over stagnation.
- **Teamwork** over turmoil.
- **Results** over reasons.
- **Implementation** over inaction.
- **Progress** over perfection.
- **Execution** over excuses.

Jerome Lewis

Jerome "Mr. Implementation" Lewis

Table of Contents

"A book is not just a book; it's the passport to your credibility, visibility, and marketability. Embrace it as your Ultimate Marketing Asset."

THE ULTIMATE
REAL ESTATE
MARKETING ASSET

Your Everlasting Marketing Asset That Will
Last A Lifetime and How You Can Use It To
Attract High-Quality Clients To Achieve
Financial Freedom and Build Wealth

*11+ Ways Real Estate Professionals Can Use a Book To Gain
More High-Quality Clients and Build A Better Real
Estate Business*

JEROME LEWIS

Read This First

I highly recommend you read this book in its entirety, but if you are looking for <u>faster results and faster solutions</u>, you can reach out to us directly to get expedited help. Continue reading and follow the process to see if you qualify.

Email directly here: **Jerome@JeromeLewis.com**

Do You Feel Like You're Shooting Arrows in the Dark?

It's quite normal to feel like you're lost when it comes to finding your target audience. It's a tough task, and it often feels like you're wasting your resources on marketing campaigns that don't bring the desired results. It's a hard cycle to break, isn't it?

Are You Struggling to Stand Out?

Even if you think you've identified your target market, there's another challenge - standing out from the crowd. The marketplace is full of competition, and it can feel like you're just one voice in a noisy room. That's overwhelming, right?

Having Trouble with Lead Generation?

Getting high-quality leads is a common hurdle. You might be getting some traffic, but those leads don't become loyal customers. This not only hurts your profits but can also make you doubt your marketing efforts.

Is Converting Leads to Sales a Challenge?

And what about turning those leads into sales? You have potential customers showing interest, but they never quite make it to the purchase. This can lead to questions about your strategies and whether they're really working.

Are You Stressed about Customer Retention?

Once you have customers, keeping them while also attracting new ones is a juggling act. Customer retention is important for the long-term growth of your business. But trying to focus on both retention and attraction can feel like too much.

The Solution: A Fractional CMO

Running a business and handling these marketing challenges can feel overwhelming. But you don't have to do it alone. The solution is hiring a Fractional CMO.

The Benefits of a Fractional CMO

A Fractional CMO is an experienced marketing expert who works part-time with your company. They bring their skills and knowledge to your team without the need for a full-time commitment. This is an effective and budget-friendly solution, especially for small and medium businesses. They can help you understand your target market, increase brand awareness, generate and convert high-quality leads, and implement successful customer retention strategies.

Ready to Take the Next Step?

If you're ready to overcome these challenges and give your business a boost, you can apply to work with me, Jerome Lewis. Just send an email to Jerome@JeromeLewis.com to start your application. Let's harness the power of a Fractional CMO to overcome your marketing challenges and grow your business together!

Best wishes,

Jerome "Mr. Implementation" Lewis

How To Get The Best Use Of This Book

This book is written in a way that can help you <u>implement</u> the strategies and suggestions within. It's *not* meant to be a long-winded book of theory.

It's meant as an <u>actionable</u> and <u>practical</u> guide that you can use to implement to gain **fast results**.

Sincerely,

Jerome "Mr. Implementation" Lewis

Introduction

Welcome, real estate professional, to an exciting journey that will revolutionize the way you do business. This is not just a book; it's an indispensable guide that's poised to become your most powerful marketing asset.

Why This Book?

The real estate industry is a competitive landscape, with a multitude of agents vying for a limited pool of clients. Standing out in such a crowded field requires innovative thinking and unique approaches. Marketing and lead generation can often seem daunting, especially for those just getting started. But what if there was a tool that could help you address these challenges?

This book is your roadmap to using a book - yes, a book - as a strategic marketing tool to transform your real estate business. If you're thinking, "I'm a real estate professional, not an author," bear with me. Writing a book may seem like an enormous task, but with the right approach, it becomes manageable and well worth the effort.

What Will You Learn?

In this book, you will learn how to establish yourself as an expert, build trust and credibility with potential clients, and generate leads that will attract new business. It will also guide you on creating new income streams, building your personal brand and network, and reducing lead generation and advertising costs.

You will discover the importance of a book in expanding your reach, how to use your book for impactful social media posts, and even how to use your book for direct mail marketing campaigns. By the time you finish reading, you will have a concrete plan to use a book as a powerful marketing tool.

Who Is This Book For?

This book is for any real estate professional who wants to elevate their business to new heights. Whether you're a seasoned veteran looking to revamp your marketing strategy or a newcomer aiming to make a splash, this book provides valuable insights that will empower you to make a lasting impact in the real estate industry.

Let's Begin!

The journey may be challenging, but remember - the view from the top is always worth the climb. Let's get started on your path to becoming a published author and a recognized expert in your field.

🔑 Key Takeaways 🔑

1. This book will guide you to use a book as a powerful marketing tool.

2. It is meant for real estate professionals seeking to elevate their business.

3. You will learn to establish expertise, generate leads, build your personal brand, and much more.

Action Item

- Approach this book with an open mind and a readiness to transform your business. Keep a notepad handy for jotting down ideas as they come. Let's dive in!

Chapter 1: Leveraging Your Ultimate Marketing Asset for Industry Expertise

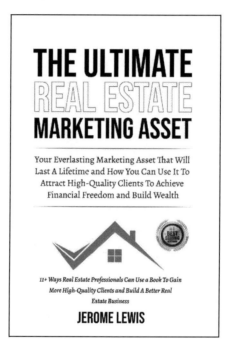

Leveraging a Book for Expertise

So, you are wondering how a book can help establish yourself as an expert in the real estate industry? Well, authoring a book offers an unrivaled opportunity to showcase your knowledge, insights, and expertise. It sends a powerful message about your credibility and authority in the industry. Let's delve into how this works.

Showcasing Your Knowledge

Writing a book about real estate allows you to present your wealth of knowledge to your audience. By providing insights on real estate trends, market analysis, investment strategies, and more, you establish yourself as an industry expert.

Illustrating Your Experience

Real-life examples and case studies add weight to your insights. By sharing your personal experiences and illustrating how you overcame challenges or capitalized on opportunities, you paint a picture of your hands-on experience in the industry.

Adding Value to Readers

The real value of a book lies in its ability to enrich its readers. When you share actionable advice and helpful tips that readers can apply, you provide value. This not only boosts your reputation but also fosters trust among your readers.

Staying Current

Keeping your content up-to-date and relevant to current market conditions underscores your active involvement and knowledge in the real estate industry. It reflects your commitment to staying abreast of industry changes, which is a key attribute of an expert.

🔑 Key Takeaways 🔑

1. Writing a book provides an excellent platform to showcase your knowledge and expertise in the real estate industry.

2. Sharing personal experiences and real-life case studies add credibility to your insights.

3. Providing actionable advice and staying current with industry trends are crucial for establishing your expertise.

Action Item

- Identify key insights, experiences, and pieces of advice that you can share in your book to underscore your expertise in the real estate industry.

Now that you have a grasp on how a book can establish your expertise, let's move on to the next chapter and explore how a book can help you build trust and credibility with potential clients. Stay tuned!

Chapter 2: Building Client Trust and Credibility with Your Ultimate Marketing Asset

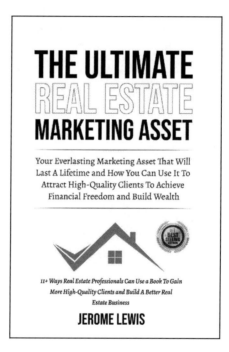

The Power of a Book in Building Trust

Let's take a look at how authoring a book can be your golden ticket to establishing credibility and fostering trust among potential clients.

Insightful Content that Resonates

When your book is filled with insightful, relevant content that addresses the common pain points in real estate, potential clients perceive you as a problem solver. They understand that you comprehend the intricacies of the industry, which increases their trust in your ability to serve their needs.

Sharing Personal Experiences

Personal stories and experiences go a long way in establishing an emotional connection with your readers. When you share your journey, including the challenges you overcame and the successes you enjoyed, it resonates with potential clients and builds trust.

Demonstration of Expertise

In-depth exploration of real estate topics, latest trends, market dynamics, etc., in your book demonstrates your expertise. When readers witness your command over these subjects, it enhances your credibility, making you a trustworthy figure in the industry.

Consistent Value Delivery

Offering consistent value to your readers helps build lasting trust. Whether it's actionable tips, data-driven insights, or thought-provoking predictions, if every chapter of your book provides value, it bolsters your reputation and credibility.

🔑 Key Takeaways 🔑

1. Insightful, relevant content that addresses common pain points builds trust.

2. Sharing personal experiences helps establish an emotional connection with potential clients.

3. Demonstrating expertise enhances your credibility.

4. Consistently delivering value bolsters your reputation.

Action Item

- Identify key real estate topics you can explore in your book to demonstrate your expertise and address common pain points.

In the next chapter, we will explore how a book can generate leads and attract new business. Stay tuned!

Chapter 3: Lead Generation and Business Attraction Using Your Ultimate Marketing Asset

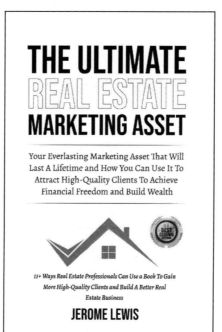

Transforming a Book into a Lead Generation Tool

How does a book transform into a tool for generating leads and attracting new business? Let's dive deeper into the process and strategies.

Delivering Value that Converts

By delivering value in your book, you can effectively convert readers into potential clients. By tackling common challenges and offering actionable solutions, you show potential clients that you can help them achieve their real estate goals.

Implementing Calls to Action

Your book is an excellent place to include calls to action (CTAs). Whether it's a prompt to contact you for a consultation, sign up for a newsletter, or follow you on social media, CTAs can transform passive readers into active leads.

Utilizing Your Book as a Freebie

Offering a free chapter, or even the entire book, in exchange for a potential client's email address can be a fantastic lead generation strategy. This tactic gives potential clients a taste of the value you can provide, making them more likely to seek your services.

🔑 Key Takeaways 🔑

1. Delivering valuable, actionable content in your book can convert readers into potential clients.

2. Implementing calls to action in your book can turn readers into leads.

3. Offering your book (or parts of it) as a freebie in exchange for contact information is a proven lead generation strategy.

Action Item

- Plan and incorporate strategic calls to action in your book, and consider how you might use your book as a "freebie" to generate leads.

In the next chapter, we'll discuss how a book can open new income streams. Let's continue on this exciting journey!

Chapter 4: Creating New Income Streams with Your Ultimate Marketing Asset

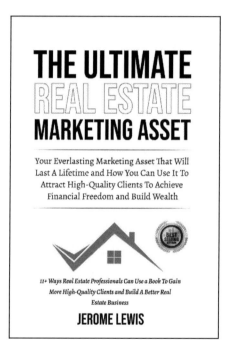

Turning a Book into a Source of Revenue

Can a book be more than just a marketing tool? Absolutely! Let's uncover the potential of a book to serve as a new income stream.

Direct Revenue from Book Sales

The most obvious income stream from a book is the revenue generated from its sales. Whether you choose to sell it online, in bookstores, at events, or through your personal network, each sale contributes to your income.

Paid Speaking Opportunities

As an author, you become a recognized authority on the subject matter. This opens up opportunities for paid speaking engagements at industry events, seminars, workshops, or webinars, where you can share your insights and promote your book.

Increased Client Consultations

A book can serve as an impressive portfolio, showcasing your knowledge and expertise. This can attract more clients to your real estate services, resulting in increased consultations and, consequently, more revenue.

Subscription-Based Exclusive Content

Your book could also serve as a gateway to more exclusive content. Readers who found your book valuable might be willing to pay for a subscription to a newsletter or blog, where they can gain access to additional insights from you.

 **Key Takeaways**

1. Revenue from book sales is a direct income stream.

2. Your book can open up opportunities for paid speaking engagements.

3. By showcasing your expertise, a book can attract more clients to your services.

Action Item

- Consider the different ways you can monetize your book and plan a marketing strategy that capitalizes on these income streams.

In the next chapter, we'll examine how a book contributes to building your personal brand. Stay tuned!

Chapter 5: Building Your Personal Brand with Your Ultimate Marketing Asset

The Role of a Book in Brand Building

A book can be an influential element of your personal brand strategy. But how does it fit into the brand-building puzzle? Let's break it down.

Communicating Your Brand's Values

Through your book, you can express your brand's values and mission. By aligning your content with these values, you ensure that your readers - potential clients - understand what you stand for in the real estate business.

Establishing Your Unique Voice

A book allows you to establish a distinct voice. Whether your style is professional, conversational, or instructive, your voice should resonate with your target audience and reflect your personal brand.

Differentiating Your Brand

A book can set you apart from other real estate professionals. It gives you the space to demonstrate your unique approach to real estate, be it your innovative tactics, your proven strategies, or your exceptional customer service.

Showcasing Expertise and Authenticity

Your book can showcase your expertise, further enhancing your personal brand. Plus, by including authentic stories and experiences, you can connect with your audience on a deeper level.

🔑 Key Takeaways 🔑

1. A book allows you to communicate your brand's values and establish your unique voice.

2. Differentiating your brand is key, and a book provides the perfect platform to do so.

3. Showcasing your expertise and authenticity through your book enhances your personal brand.

Action Item

- Identify the values and unique aspects of your personal brand that you want to communicate through your book.

Stay tuned for the next chapter, where we'll discuss how a book can help in building your network. Onward to more insights!

Chapter 6: Networking in Real Estate through Your Ultimate Marketing Asset

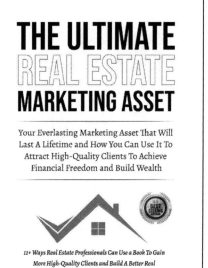

The Networking Power of a Book

A book isn't just for readers. It's also a powerful networking tool. Let's delve into how a book can help expand your professional network.

Breaking the Ice

A book can serve as an excellent conversation starter, breaking the ice at networking events or during meetings with other industry professionals. It also provides a common ground to kick-start meaningful discussions.

Connecting with Influencers

You can use your book as a tool to reach out to influencers and industry leaders. Sending them a copy of your book with a personalized note can get the conversation started and potentially lead to new relationships and collaborations.

Building Relationships with Readers

Your book opens up an avenue for two-way communication with your readers. Engage with them on social media, at book signings, or via email to transform readers into connections.

Collaborating with Other Authors

Reaching out to other authors for joint ventures, like webinars, podcasts, or co-authoring a blog post, can also help expand your network.

🗝 Key Takeaways 🗝

1. A book can act as a conversation starter at networking events.

2. Your book can help you connect with influencers and industry leaders.

3. Engaging with your readers can help build relationships and expand your network.

4. Collaborating with other authors can lead to joint ventures and broader network expansion.

Action Item

- Identify networking opportunities where your book can act as an icebreaker or medium for engagement.

The journey continues in the next chapter, where we'll explore how a book can help in generating more leads. Stay tuned!

Chapter 7: Lead Generation Strategies Using Your Ultimate Marketing Asset

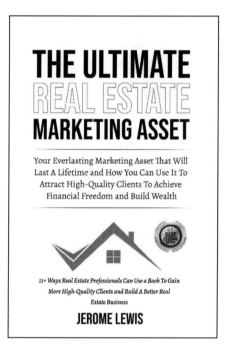

The Lead-Generation Potential of a Book

If you've ever wondered how a book can help generate leads, you're in for a treat. Let's delve into the strategies you can utilize.

A Business Card on Steroids

Think of your book as a business card on steroids. It provides prospective clients with a detailed look into your knowledge and expertise in the real estate market, making them more likely to contact you for their needs.

Driving Traffic to Your Website

Including your website link in your book is a smart way to drive traffic. By offering additional resources, such as blog articles, guides, or even exclusive property listings, you can encourage readers to visit your site.

Providing a Contact Form in Your Book

Consider including a contact form at the end of your book or at the end of each chapter. This gives interested readers a quick and easy way to reach out, transforming them into potential leads.

Leveraging Email Marketing

By offering a free digital copy or a chapter of your book in exchange for an email address, you can grow your email list. This enables you to stay connected with potential clients and keep them informed about your services.

🔑 Key Takeaways 🔑

- Think of your book as a powerful business card that demonstrates your expertise.

- Drive traffic to your website by including your link in your book.

- Incorporate a contact form in your book to transform readers into potential leads.

- Offer a free digital copy or a chapter of your book in exchange for email addresses to bolster your email marketing.

Action Item

- Devise strategies to integrate lead-generation tactics into your book's content and promotional efforts.

In the next chapter, we'll discover how a book can aid in establishing your credibility. Onwards to more insights!

Chapter 8: Establishing Real Estate Credibility with Your Ultimate Marketing Asset

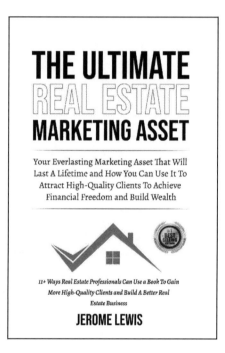

The Credibility Quotient of a Book

In an industry where credibility is king, a book can serve as your crown. Let's examine how a book can enhance your credibility in the real estate field.

Showcasing In-Depth Knowledge

A book allows you to demonstrate your extensive knowledge of the real estate industry. Readers will appreciate your insights and perceive you as a trusted expert.

Highlighting Case Studies

Including case studies of your past successes in your book can further bolster your credibility. Real-world examples of how you've helped clients achieve their real estate goals will reinforce your reputation as a competent and effective professional.

Garnering Reviews and Testimonials

Reviews and testimonials can serve as powerful endorsements of your credibility. Encourage readers to leave reviews on your book's sales page and include testimonials from satisfied clients.

Being a Published Author

Being a published author alone carries significant weight. It implies you have a level of expertise and knowledge that warranted writing a book, enhancing your credibility among clients and industry peers.

🔑 Key Takeaways 🔑

1. Showcasing your in-depth knowledge through a book enhances your credibility.

2. Case studies provide tangible proof of your capabilities and success in the real estate industry.

3. Reviews and testimonials can serve as powerful endorsements of your credibility.

4. The status of being a published author boosts your credibility.

Action Item

- Identify successful case studies, reviews, and testimonials that you can include in your book to demonstrate your credibility.

In the next chapter, we'll delve into how a book can help expand your reach. Stay tuned for more insights!

Chapter 9: Expanding Your Reach in Real Estate with Your Ultimate Marketing Asset

Unfolding the Reach of a Book

A book isn't just a compilation of pages; it's a tool that can expand your reach beyond geographical boundaries. Let's unravel the reach of a book.

Building an Online Presence

By listing your book on online platforms, you gain visibility among a global audience. This not only increases your reach but also opens up opportunities to connect with international clients.

Gaining Media Exposure

A book can catch the attention of media outlets, leading to interviews or features that can significantly increase your visibility. This exposure can bring new readers and potential clients into your sphere of influence.

Reaching Out to Libraries and Bookstores

Libraries and bookstores are still frequented by many people. Having your book available in these places can expand your reach to potential clients who prefer traditional reading methods.

Leveraging Affiliate Marketing

You can partner with affiliates who can promote your book to their audience. This way, your reach extends to their followers or subscribers, bringing in new potential leads.

🔑 Key Takeaways 🔑

1. Listing your book online can increase your reach and visibility.

2. Media exposure through your book can attract new readers and potential clients.

3. Libraries and bookstores provide another avenue to reach potential clients.

4. Affiliate marketing can help extend your book's reach.

Action Item

- Identify online platforms, media outlets, libraries, and potential affiliates who can help you expand your book's reach.

Up next, we'll learn how a book can assist in building your brand. Stay tuned for more insights!

Chapter 10: Building a Powerful Real Estate Brand with Your Ultimate Marketing Asset

Unfolding the Reach of a Book

A book isn't just a compilation of pages; it's a tool that can expand your reach beyond geographical boundaries. Let's unravel the reach of a book.

Building an Online Presence

By listing your book on online platforms, you gain visibility among a global audience. This not only increases your reach but also opens up opportunities to connect with international clients.

Gaining Media Exposure

A book can catch the attention of media outlets, leading to interviews or features that can significantly increase your visibility. This exposure can bring new readers and potential clients into your sphere of influence.

Reaching Out to Libraries and Bookstores

Libraries and bookstores are still frequented by many people. Having your book available in these places can expand your reach to potential clients who prefer traditional reading methods.

Leveraging Affiliate Marketing

You can partner with affiliates who can promote your book to their audience. This way, your reach extends to their followers or subscribers, bringing in new potential leads.

🔑 Key Takeaways 🔑

- Listing your book online can increase your reach and visibility.

- Media exposure through your book can attract new readers and potential clients.

- Libraries and bookstores provide another avenue to reach potential clients.

- Affiliate marketing can help extend your book's reach.

Action Item

- Identify online platforms, media outlets, libraries, and potential affiliates who can help you expand your book's reach.

Up next, we'll learn how a book can assist in building your brand. Stay tuned for more insights!

Chapter 11: How Can the Ultimate Marketing Asset Contribute to Building a Strong Brand in Real Estate?

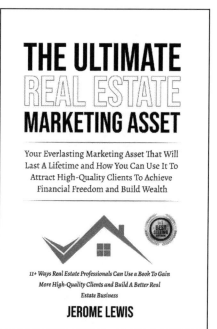

The Brand Building Power of a Book

Your brand is your promise to your clients. It differentiates your offering from others in the market. Let's explore how a book can enhance this brand building process.

Communicating Your Brand Philosophy

Your book provides a medium to communicate your brand philosophy. You can share your principles, vision, and commitment, giving readers a deeper understanding of what your brand represents.

Showcasing Your Unique Selling Proposition

What sets you apart from other real estate professionals? Your book can showcase your unique selling proposition (USP), strengthening your brand's position in the market.

Creating a Personal Connection

Your book allows you to tell your story, create a personal connection with readers, and portray the human side of your brand. This can generate trust and loyalty, key elements for successful brand building.

Promoting Your Brand Consistently

Consistency is key in branding. Ensure that your book's tone, style, and message align with your overall brand communication. This consistency reinforces your brand image in the minds of your readers.

🔑 Key Takeaways 🔑

1. Your book is a tool to communicate your brand philosophy.

2. A book allows you to showcase your unique selling proposition.

3. Use your book to create a personal connection with readers, enhancing brand loyalty.

4. Consistency across your book and your overall brand communication is essential in reinforcing your brand image.

Action Item

- Reflect on your brand philosophy, USP, and overall brand communication strategy. Identify how these elements can be effectively conveyed through your book.

In the next chapter, we'll discover how a book can help in reducing lead generation and advertising costs. Stay tuned!

Chapter 12: Reducing Costs with Your Ultimate Marketing Asset

THE ULTIMATE
REAL ESTATE
MARKETING ASSET

Your Everlasting Marketing Asset That Will
Last A Lifetime and How You Can Use It To
Attract High-Quality Clients To Achieve
Financial Freedom and Build Wealth

*11+ Ways Real Estate Professionals Can Use a Book To Gain
More High-Quality Clients and Build A Better Real
Estate Business*

JEROME LEWIS

Economizing with a Book

While traditional advertising can be costly, a book can be a cost-effective tool for lead generation and advertising. Let's delve into how.

Organic Lead Generation

A book acts as a magnet for organic leads. Readers who find value in your content are likely to reach out for your services, reducing the need for paid lead generation efforts.

Word-of-Mouth Marketing

A well-written, insightful book can stimulate word-of-mouth marketing. Satisfied readers may recommend your book (and by extension, your services) to their networks, resulting in free advertising.

Long-Term Visibility

Traditional advertisements have a limited lifespan, whereas a book offers long-term visibility. Your book continues to advertise your services long after its release, offering a high return on investment.

Building a Mailing List

By offering a free digital copy or a chapter of your book in exchange for email addresses, you can build a mailing list without additional advertising costs.

🔑 Key Takeaways 🔑

1. A book can serve as a magnet for organic leads, reducing the need for costly paid lead generation.

2. A well-crafted book can stimulate word-of-mouth marketing, providing free advertising.

3. Your book provides long-term visibility, offering a high return on investment compared to traditional ads.

4. You can build a mailing list without additional advertising costs by offering a part of your book in exchange for email addresses.

Action Item

- Consider strategies to maximize your book's potential for organic lead generation, word-of-mouth marketing, and building a mailing list.

In the next chapter, we'll explore how to use your book for social media posts. Keep reading for more insights!

Chapter 13: How Can You Use Your Ultimate Marketing Asset for Social Media Posts?

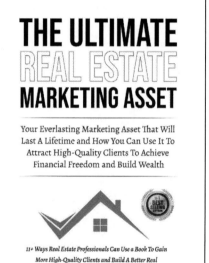

Social Media and Your Book: The Connection

Social media offers a great platform to amplify your book's reach. Here's how to leverage your book content for engaging social media posts.

Sharing Snippets

Share snippets from your book as social media posts to intrigue your audience and pique their interest in your full book.

Creating Quote Graphics

Transform memorable quotes from your book into eye-catching graphics. These can be easily shared and have the potential to go viral, increasing your visibility.

Hosting Book Discussions

Host live book discussions on platforms like Facebook or Instagram. These interactive sessions can engage your followers and spark conversations around your book's content.

Sharing Testimonials

Share testimonials from readers who found value in your book. This can foster trust in potential readers and inspire them to pick up a copy.

Offering Giveaways

Run a social media giveaway contest with your book as the prize. This can increase engagement and visibility, attracting more potential leads.

🔑 Key Takeaways 🔑

1. Sharing snippets from your book can attract potential readers.

2. Quote graphics are shareable content that can increase your book's visibility.

3. Hosting book discussions on social media can engage your audience.

4. Sharing testimonials can encourage potential readers to check out your book.

5. Giveaway contests can enhance your book's visibility and bring in potential leads.

Action Item

- Create a social media content calendar leveraging various aspects of your book and schedule posts to engage with your audience effectively.

Stay tuned for the next chapter where we'll delve into how your book can be used for direct mail marketing campaigns!

Chapter 14: How Can You Use Your Ultimate Marketing Asset for Direct Mail Marketing Campaigns?

Direct Mail and Your Book: The Perfect Pair

In an age of digital communication, direct mail can stand out. Here's how to use your book effectively in direct mail marketing campaigns.

Offering a Free Book

A free book can make for an exciting and valuable piece of direct mail. It stands out in the pile of regular mail and encourages the recipient to engage with your brand.

Sending Personalized Letters

Include a personalized letter with your book. Share why you believe the recipient will find your book helpful and how it relates to their real estate needs.

Creating a Book Catalog

If you've written multiple books, a catalog can be an effective piece of direct mail. It gives recipients an overview of your offerings and can pique their interest in your other books.

Using Postcards

A postcard featuring your book cover and a compelling call to action can be a cost-effective direct mail option. It can drive recipients to your website or online store to learn more about your book.

🔑 Key Takeaways 🔑

1. Offering a free book as direct mail can help you stand out and engage recipients.

2. Personalized letters along with your book can establish a personal connection with the recipient.

3. A book catalog can pique interest in your other books.

4. Postcards with your book cover can direct recipients to your website or online store.

Action Item

-   Plan out a direct mail campaign, deciding whether you'll offer a free book, personalized letters, a catalog, or postcards.

In the next chapter, we'll learn how to use your book to boost your newsletter subscribers. Stay tuned for more insights!

Chapter 14: Boosting Newsletter Subscriptions with Your Ultimate Marketing Asset

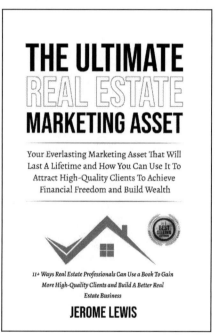

Amplifying Your Mailing List Through Your Book

A robust mailing list is a valuable asset for any business. Let's discover how your book can help you boost your newsletter subscribers.

Offering a Free Chapter

Offering the first chapter of your book for free in exchange for a newsletter subscription can attract new subscribers. This provides value to the subscriber while also piquing their interest in your book.

Inviting Readers to Join Your Newsletter

Include an invitation to join your newsletter within your book. Make sure to communicate the benefits the reader will get from your newsletter, such as industry insights, tips, or exclusive offers.

Running a Subscription Contest

Consider running a contest where new newsletter subscribers can win a free copy of your book. This can incentivize sign-ups and grow your mailing list.

Using QR Codes

Incorporate a QR code in your book that leads to your newsletter sign-up page. This provides an easy, seamless way for readers to subscribe.

 Key Takeaways

1. Offering a free chapter of your book can attract new newsletter subscribers.

2. An invitation to join your newsletter within your book can convert readers into subscribers.

3. Subscription contests can incentivize newsletter sign-ups.

4. QR codes in your book can provide an easy way for readers to subscribe to your newsletter.

Action Item

- Plan how you will use your book to boost newsletter subscribers, considering options like a free chapter, a direct invitation, a subscription contest, or a QR code.

Next, we'll unlock the secrets of fast book writing. Keep reading for more tips and insights!

Chapter 15: Fast Writing Secrets for Your Ultimate Marketing Asset

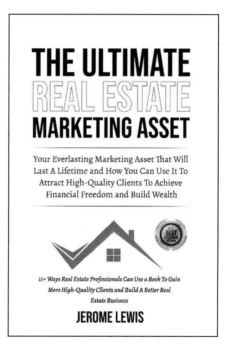

Accelerating Your Book Writing Process

Writing a book can be a daunting task, but it doesn't have to be. Let's uncover the secrets to fast book writing.

Setting Clear Goals

Having a clear understanding of what you want to achieve with your book can help streamline the writing process. Clearly define your book's purpose, audience, and key messages.

Creating an Outline

An outline serves as a roadmap for your book. It breaks down the book into manageable parts and can significantly speed up the writing process.

Writing Every Day

Establish a regular writing routine. Even a small amount of daily writing can add up over time, helping you make significant progress.

Minimizing Distractions

Find a quiet, comfortable place to write and eliminate potential distractions. This can help you stay focused and increase your writing speed.

Hiring a Ghostwriter

If you're struggling with the writing process, consider hiring a ghostwriter. They can help bring your ideas to life while saving you time.

 Key Takeaways

1. Setting clear goals can streamline your book writing process.

2. Creating an outline can speed up your writing.

3. Regular daily writing can help you make significant progress on your book.

4. Minimizing distractions can increase your writing speed.

5. Hiring a ghostwriter can save you time and help bring your ideas to life.

Action Item

- Plan out your book writing strategy, considering your goals, writing routine, work environment, and whether you might benefit from a ghostwriter.

In the next chapter, we'll wrap things up and look at what comes next after your book is written. Keep reading for the conclusion!

Chapter 16: Conclusion - The Power of Your Ultimate Marketing Asset

Reflecting on the Journey

As we conclude our journey of understanding how a book can become a powerful marketing tool, let's revisit the key concepts we've covered.

Establishing Expertise and Credibility

We began by learning how writing a book helps establish you as an expert in the real estate industry, building trust and credibility with potential clients.

Lead Generation and Branding

We discovered how a book can generate leads, attract new business, and create new income streams. We also discussed how it aids in building your personal brand and network.

Marketing Tactics

We delved into marketing tactics, understanding how a book can reduce lead generation and advertising costs, how to use it for social media posts, direct mail campaigns, and boosting newsletter subscriptions.

Accelerated Writing

Lastly, we explored tips to accelerate the book writing process, highlighting the importance of setting clear goals, writing daily, minimizing distractions, and possibly hiring a ghostwriter.

🔑 Key Takeaways 🔑

- A book can establish your expertise and credibility in the real estate industry.

- It serves as a powerful tool for lead generation, branding, and creating new income streams.

- Your book can enhance your marketing efforts, reducing costs, and increasing reach.

- There are strategies to speed up the book writing process, making it less daunting and more achievable.

Action Item

- Reflect on the lessons learned and start planning your book writing and marketing journey, keeping in mind the tactics and strategies we've discussed.

As we move on to the final chapter, let's discuss the next steps you can take after your book is written. Keep reading for more!

Chapter 17: Next Steps - Leveraging Your Ultimate Marketing Asset for Success

The Obstacle of Modern Real Estate: Frustration and Uncertainty

Are you a real estate professional frustrated with your current marketing efforts? Maybe you're finding it challenging to generate qualified leads and close deals. You know that growing your business requires robust marketing strategies, but you're not sure where to begin or how to improve. You're not alone - these are common challenges that many real estate professionals face.

Amplifying Your Struggles: The Impact on Your Business

These issues can be incredibly frustrating. You've likely spent countless hours trying various marketing tactics, only to see little return on your investment. The lack of qualified leads and closed deals might have left you feeling uncertain about the future of your business. Moreover, the constant pressure to grow and the uncertainty can be stressful and overwhelming.

Your Path to Success: A Unique Marketing Strategy

But it doesn't have to be this way. What if you had a comprehensive, step-by-step guide to leverage an unconventional yet powerful marketing tool - a book. A tool that not only establishes your expertise and credibility but also generates leads, creates new income streams, builds your personal brand, and network, ultimately growing your real estate business.

And you're holding that guide in your hands.

Over the last 16 chapters, we've laid out the process of using a book as a marketing asset in detail. But the journey doesn't end here.

Embrace the Change: Connect with Jerome Lewis

I, Jerome Lewis, the author of this book, am here to help you put these principles into action. I can guide you through each step of leveraging your book as a powerful marketing tool.

Contact me at Jerome@JeromeLewis.com. Let's discuss how you can overcome your marketing frustrations, generate more leads, close more deals, and grow your real estate business exponentially. Let's turn the page to the next chapter of your success story.

Your journey to becoming a renowned expert in the real estate industry and growing your business beyond expectations starts with a single step. Reach out today. Your future self will thank you.

🔑 Key Takeaways 🔑

1. Many real estate professionals struggle with marketing, lead generation, and closing deals.

2. These challenges can be frustrating and detrimental to business growth.

3. Leveraging a book as a marketing tool can help overcome these challenges.

4. The author, Jerome Lewis, is available to guide you through this process.

Action Item

- Reach out to Jerome Lewis at Jerome@JeromeLewis.com to start your journey towards overcoming marketing challenges and growing your real estate business.

★Bonus: Implementation Checklist

☐ Approach this book with an open mind and a readiness to transform your business. Keep a notepad handy for jotting down ideas as they come. Let's dive in!

☐ Begin brainstorming about your personal experiences, skills, and knowledge in real estate that you can use to establish yourself as an expert.

☐ Identify three key areas where you can start building trust and credibility with your potential clients.

☐ Develop a strategy on how to use your upcoming book as a tool for lead generation and attracting new business.

☐ Consider new income streams that your book could potentially create and start planning how to implement them.

☐ Start thinking about your personal brand – how do you want to be perceived by your readers and clients? How can your book help enhance this image?

☐ Brainstorm ways to use your book to expand your network – consider who you want in your network and how your book can attract them.

☐ Design a plan for using your book to generate leads – who are your target readers and how can your book entice them to become leads?

☐ Identify areas in your business where you need to establish more credibility, and consider how your book can help achieve this.

☐ Plan a strategy to use your book to expand your reach – who is your target audience and how can your book reach them?

☐ Start planning how your book can contribute to building your brand – what aspects of your brand can be enhanced or showcased in your book?

☐ Consider ways you can reduce lead generation and advertising costs using your book – perhaps through social media promotion, email marketing, or other cost-effective strategies.

☐ Plan out your social media strategy for promoting your book – consider which platforms are most suitable for your audience and what kind of content you will share.

☐ Draft a direct mail campaign plan using your book as a marketing tool.

☐ Develop a strategy for using your book to boost your newsletter subscribers.

☐ Plan out your book writing strategy, considering your goals, writing routine, work environment, and whether you might benefit from a ghostwriter.

☐ Reflect on the lessons learned and start planning your book writing and marketing journey, keeping in mind the tactics and strategies we've discussed.

☐ Reach out to Jerome Lewis at Jerome@JeromeLewis.com to start your journey towards overcoming marketing challenges and growing your real estate business.

Bonus: The Ultimate Marketing Asset - Write, Publish, Market – Harness the Power of a Book for Your Business

"The person who <u>does not</u> read has no advantage over the person who *cannot* read." - Mark Twain

An old saying goes, "Everyone has a book inside them." But few realize that a book is not just a medium to share your story or insights; it can be one of the most effective marketing tools for your business.

Your Book as a Lead Magnet

When you think about a lead magnet, a free PDF or an e-newsletter might come to mind. But a book? It's a game-changer. Offering your book as a lead magnet is a powerful way to collect customer information. You provide valuable content, and in return, you get the contact details of potential customers. It's a win-win scenario that sets the stage for a deeper relationship with your audience.

Decrease Advertising Spend

Your book isn't just a lead magnet—it's also a brilliant way to decrease your advertising spend. Instead of investing heavily in various advertising platforms, you can allow customers to purchase your book. This purchase not only offsets some of your marketing costs but also builds a more personal and stronger connection with your audience than traditional advertising.

A Marketing Asset That Stays

Unlike flyers or brochures that people tend to discard, books have staying power. People rarely throw away books. They sit on bookshelves, travel in bags, and often get passed from person to person. Your book, carrying your name and ideas, becomes a long-lasting marketing asset that constantly works for you.

Leverage Videos, Transcripts, and AI

You may think, "But writing a book is a herculean task!" It's true if you're imagining yourself locked in a room, typing away for months. However, anybody can write a book by leveraging videos, transcripts, and AI. By using the technology available to us, we can streamline the process and make it more manageable. Create video content, transcribe it, correct and edit with AI tools, and voila - you're on your way to becoming an author!

🔑 Key Takeaways 🔑

1. Your book can be an effective lead magnet, enabling you to collect valuable customer information.

2. By using your book as a marketing tool, you can decrease your advertising spend.

3. A book is a marketing asset with longevity - people do not throw books away.

4. Leveraging videos, transcripts, and AI can simplify the book-writing process.

🔧 Implementation 🔧

It's time to spring into action! If you're passionate about amplifying your business impact and sharing your unique insights through a book, I'm here to guide you through the process. The world is eager for your unique perspective, and there's no better moment to start sharing them.

Why not take the first step today? Drop me an email at Jerome@JeromeLewis.com to schedule a call. Let's embark on your book-writing journey together, efficiently and effectively!

⭐Bonus: The Need for Speed: Harnessing Quick Wins in Marketing

"Success in marketing doesn't wait for those who stall. It's the swift who seize the moment, transforming challenges into opportunities with velocity."

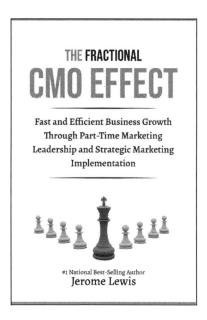

Why Speed Matters in Marketing

In today's fast-paced digital world, speed is no longer a luxury; it's a necessity. Your potential customers are constantly bombarded with advertisements and promotions from every corner. They're making decisions in real-time and if your business isn't quick to the punch, you could lose out.

The Benefits of Rapid Implementation

Speed brings the advantage of rapid implementation. This means getting your marketing campaigns off the ground quickly, allowing you to reach your customers before your competition does. This allows you to collect data, evaluate performance, and refine your strategy much faster. The faster you operate, the more opportunities you have to test, fail, learn, and succeed.

Agility in Decision-Making

Hiring a Fractional CMO brings with it the benefit of agility. These experienced marketing executives are skilled at making informed decisions quickly. This means that instead of waiting for the next board meeting to discuss a potential marketing strategy, a Fractional CMO can analyze the situation and make a call right away, keeping your business ahead of the curve.

Speed to Market

In marketing, the early bird often gets the worm. By being quick to market with a new product or a promotional offer, you can capture the attention of consumers before your competitors do. A Fractional CMO can help you devise and implement these quick-to-market strategies, gaining you an edge in a competitive market.

Quick Adaptation to Market Changes

Markets change, and they change fast. A successful business is one that can pivot quickly to adapt to these changes. With a Fractional CMO on board, you can quickly adjust your marketing strategies to cater to new market trends, ensuring that your business remains relevant and engaging to your target audience.

Conclusion

Speed can be the deciding factor between a business that thrives and one that barely survives in today's market. By hiring a Fractional CMO, you bring on board the expertise and agility needed to make quick decisions, implement rapid strategies, and stay ahead of the competition.

Key Takeaways

1. In today's fast-paced digital world, speed is a necessity in marketing.

2. A Fractional CMO brings with them the advantage of rapid implementation and agility in decision-making.

3. The ability to adapt quickly to market changes is critical in keeping your business relevant and engaging.

🔧 Implementation

Assess your current marketing strategies. Are there areas where you could increase speed without compromising on quality? If you find this challenging, consider the benefits a Fractional CMO could bring to your business in terms of speed and efficiency.

⭐Bonus: The Game-Changer – Embracing AI in Marketing

"Artificial Intelligence does not replace human intelligence. It amplifies it. Together, we can reach new frontiers."

Understanding Artificial Intelligence (AI)

Artificial Intelligence (AI) has rapidly emerged as a transformative technology. But what exactly is it? At its core, AI is a series of technologies capable of mimicking human intelligence. It's a broad term that encompasses machine learning, natural language processing, robotics, and more. This revolutionary technology is changing the game in countless industries, including marketing.

Why AI Matters in Marketing

AI has the power to supercharge marketing efforts. It can analyze vast amounts of data faster than any human ever could. This allows companies to gain deep insights about their customers, helping them to create highly personalized experiences.

AI also automates repetitive tasks, freeing up marketers' time so they can focus on more strategic initiatives. From automated email campaigns to chatbots handling customer queries, AI is becoming a crucial part of the marketer's toolkit.

Harnessing AI for Customer Insight

One of the biggest benefits of AI in marketing is its ability to dive deep into customer data. It can identify patterns and trends that humans might overlook, helping you better understand your customers.

Using AI, you can gain insights into what your customers truly want and need. This helps you create more targeted, personalized marketing campaigns that resonate with your audience.

AI and Predictive Analytics

Predictive analytics is another area where AI shines. It can sift through data and identify future trends, allowing you to stay one step ahead. With AI, you can predict which marketing tactics will resonate best with your audience and adjust your strategy accordingly.

Embracing AI in Your Marketing Efforts

Incorporating AI into your marketing efforts can seem daunting, but it's an investment that can yield significant results. To start, identify areas where AI can have the most impact. Whether it's customer insights, automation, or predictive analytics, AI can supercharge your marketing efforts.

Remember, AI isn't here to replace marketers, but rather to augment their abilities. By leveraging AI, you can make smarter decisions, craft more effective campaigns, and ultimately drive business growth.

Key Takeaways

1. AI has the power to transform marketing, offering deep customer insights, automating tasks, and providing predictive analytics.

2. By harnessing AI, marketers can craft personalized, impactful campaigns that truly resonate with their audience.

3. Embracing AI is not about replacing humans, but about augmenting their capabilities, allowing for smarter, more effective marketing strategies.

🔧 Implementation 🔧

Identify one area of your marketing strategy where AI could have the most impact. Begin researching tools and platforms that utilize AI in this area and consider implementing them into your strategy.

⭐ Bonus: Amplifying Your Message – The Power of Video Communication

"The power of video communication is the ability to bring your message to life, engaging hearts and minds in a way that words alone cannot."

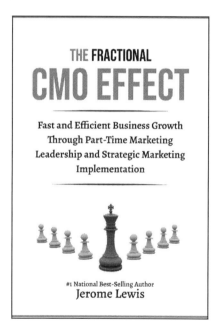

The Rise of Video Communication

In today's digital age, video has emerged as a powerful communication tool. Whether it's a viral social media clip, an engaging product demo, or a comprehensive training video, visual content is reshaping how we connect, communicate, and convey information.

Why Video Communication is Crucial in Marketing

Video communication offers numerous advantages in marketing. Its ability to convey complex messages in an engaging, digestible format can significantly enhance your marketing efforts. Here's why:

1. Enhanced Engagement

Video content is inherently engaging. It can combine visual imagery, audio, and text, creating a rich, immersive experience. This multi-sensory approach helps keep audiences engaged, making them more likely to absorb your message.

2. Improved Information Retention

Studies show that viewers retain 95% of a message when they watch it in a video, compared to 10% when reading it in text. If you want your message to stick, video is the way to go.

3. Boosts Conversion Rates

Video can help persuade potential customers to take action. According to a study by Wyzowl, 84% of people say that they've been convinced to buy a product or service by watching a brand's video.

Using Video Communication Effectively

While the benefits of video communication are clear, it's important to use it effectively. Here are some strategies:

1. Be Authentic

Authenticity resonates with audiences. Don't be afraid to show the human side of your business. This can foster trust and loyalty among your audience.

2. Keep it Short and Sweet

With the abundance of content available, attention spans are short. Keep your videos concise and to the point. Deliver your message effectively, without unnecessary fluff.

3. Use a Strong Call-to-Action

Don't forget to include a clear call-to-action. Whether it's visiting your website, signing up for a newsletter, or making a purchase, guide your viewers on what to do next.

The Future is Video

Video communication is here to stay. As technology continues to evolve, we can only expect video to become an even more integral part of our communication landscape. By harnessing the power of video, you can amplify your message and make your marketing efforts more impactful.

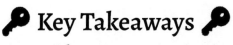 Key Takeaways

1. Video communication is a powerful tool in marketing, known for its high engagement,

improved information retention, and conversion rates.

2. To use video effectively, ensure authenticity, keep content concise, and use strong calls-to-action.

3. The future of communication is increasingly shifting towards video, making it a crucial component of any modern marketing strategy.

🔧 Implementation 🔧

Identify one key message or campaign in your marketing strategy that could benefit from being communicated through video. Start planning a short, authentic video that conveys this message, and includes a clear call-to-action for viewers.

⭐ Bonus: Navigating the Digital Landscape: The Role of Technology in Modern Business

"Embracing technology is not about abandoning tradition, it's about crafting a future where innovation fuels growth and broadens the horizons of possibility."

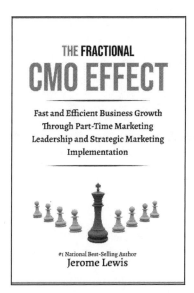

Introduction

Technology has swiftly become the backbone of nearly every industry. From the ways we communicate and market to the systems that keep our businesses running smoothly, it's hard to imagine a world without the conveniences that technology offers. In this chapter, we will explore the vital role technology plays in modern business and how it can be harnessed for greater success.

Technology: The Great Enabler

Technology is an enabler, a tool that broadens our capabilities and allows us to achieve more with less. It transforms manual processes into automated ones, freeing up time and resources. From managing finances with accounting software to reaching customers worldwide through digital marketing platforms, technology is truly a game-changer for businesses.

Communication in the Digital Era

Technology has revolutionized communication. With tools like email, video conferencing, and instant messaging, we can connect with colleagues and customers alike, no matter where in the world they might be. This ease of communication opens up a world of opportunities for collaboration and customer engagement.

Data-Driven Decision-Making

In the era of big data, technology provides us with the means to gather and analyze information on an unprecedented scale. With data analytics tools, businesses can make informed decisions based on real-time insights, leading to more effective strategies and better business outcomes.

Staying Ahead of the Curve

The pace of technological change is rapid, and businesses must adapt to stay relevant. It's crucial to keep abreast of emerging technologies and trends and to be open to integrating them into your business operations. A forward-thinking approach to technology can give your business a competitive edge.

The Future is Here

Technology is not just shaping the future; it's shaping the present. As businesses, we must embrace it, harness its power, and use it to propel us toward our goals. From improving efficiency and productivity to enabling innovative marketing strategies, technology is the key to thriving in the modern business landscape.

Key Takeaways

1. Technology is a powerful tool that can enhance various aspects of business, from communication to decision-making.

2. Embracing technology and staying updated on emerging trends is crucial for maintaining a competitive edge.

3. Leveraging technology effectively can lead to improved efficiency, better customer engagement, and ultimately, business growth.

🔧 Implementation 🔧

Identify one area in your business where technology could make a significant impact. Research and implement a tech solution that will enhance that aspect of your operations. Remember, the goal is to work smarter, not harder.

1. "If you are the kind of person who is waiting for the 'right' thing to happen, you might wait for a long time. It's like waiting for all the traffic lights to be green for five miles before starting the trip." "Often, in the real world, it's not the smart who get ahead but the bold." "The richest people in the world look for and build networks; everyone else looks for work." "When times are bad is when the real entrepreneurs emerge." "If you avoid failure, you also avoid success." "Critics only make you stronger. You have to look at what they are saying as feedback. Sometimes the feedback helps, and other times, it's just noise that can be a distraction." "The thing most people don't pick up when they become an entrepreneur is that it never ends. It's 24/7." "You have to look for teachers. If you want to be a mechanic, go hang out with mechanics." "I believe that one key to success is to accept truth – no matter how it's spoken." "Quitting is the easiest thing to do." "Inside every problem lies an opportunity." "Face your fears and doubts, and new worlds will open to

you." "I wasn't born a natural entrepreneur. I had to be trained." "Sometimes the hardest thing to do is to trust your team. It's a lesson I've had to relearn quite a few times." "Success is not a stop sign." "Most businesses think that product is the most important thing, but without great leadership, mission, and a team that delivers results at a high level, even the best product won't make a company successful."

—Robert T. Kiyosaki, Entrepreneur, Author, Investor

 If you are the kind of person who is waiting for the 'right' thing to happen, you might wait for a long time. It's like waiting for all the traffic lights to be green for five miles before starting the trip."

2. "Often, in the real world, it's not the smart who get ahead but the bold."

3. "The richest people in the world look for and build networks; everyone else looks for work."

4. "When times are bad is when the real entrepreneurs emerge."

5. "If you avoid failure, you also avoid success."

6. "Critics only make you stronger. You have to look at what they are saying as feedback. Sometimes the feedback helps, and other times, it's just noise that can be a distraction."

7.

8. "The thing most people don't pick up when they become an entrepreneur is that it never ends. It's 24/7."

9. "You have to look for teachers. If you want to be a mechanic, go hang out with mechanics."

10. "I believe that one key to success is to accept truth – no matter how it's spoken."

11. "Quitting is the easiest thing to do."

12. "Inside every problem lies an opportunity."

13. "Face your fears and doubts, and new worlds will open to you."

14. "I wasn't born a natural entrepreneur. I had to be trained."

15. "Sometimes the hardest thing to do is to trust your team. It's a lesson I've had to relearn quite a few times."

16. "Success is not a stop sign."

17. "Most businesses think that product is the most important thing, but without great leadership, mission, and a team that delivers results at a high level, even the best product won't make a company successful." —Robert T. Kiyosaki, Entrepreneur, Author, Investor"If you are the kind of person who is waiting for the 'right' thing to happen, you might wait for a long time. It's like waiting for all the traffic lights to be green for five miles before starting the trip."

"Often, in the real world, it's not the smart who get ahead but the bold." "The richest people in the world look for and build networks; everyone else looks for work." "When times are bad is when the real entrepreneurs emerge." "If you avoid failure, you also avoid success." "Critics only make you stronger. You have to look at what they are saying as feedback. Sometimes the feedback helps, and other times, it's just noise that can be a distraction." "The thing most people don't pick up when they become an entrepreneur is that it never ends. It's 24/7." "You have to look for teachers. If you want to be a mechanic, go hang out with mechanics." "I believe that one key to success is to accept truth – no matter how it's spoken." "Quitting is the easiest thing to do." "Inside every problem lies an opportunity." "Face your fears and doubts, and new worlds will open to you." "I wasn't born a natural entrepreneur. I had to be trained." "Sometimes the hardest thing to do is to trust your team. It's a lesson I've had to relearn quite a few times." "Success is not a stop sign." "Most businesses think that product is the most important thing, but without great leadership, mission, and a team that delivers results at a high level, even the best product won't make a company successful."

—Robert T. Kiyosaki, Entrepreneur, Author, Investor

1. "If you are the kind of person who is waiting for the 'right' thing to happen, you might wait for a long time. It's like waiting for all the traffic lights to be green for five miles before starting the trip."

2. "Often, in the real world, it's not the smart who get ahead but the bold."

3. "The richest people in the world look for and build networks; everyone else looks for work."

4. "When times are bad is when the real entrepreneurs emerge."

5. "If you avoid failure, you also avoid success."

6. "Critics only make you stronger. You have to look at what they are saying as feedback. Sometimes the feedback helps, and other times, it's just noise that can be a distraction."

7.

8. "The thing most people don't pick up when they become an entrepreneur is that it never ends. It's 24/7."

9. "You have to look for teachers. If you want to be a mechanic, go hang out with mechanics."

10. "I believe that one key to success is to accept truth – no matter how it's spoken."

11. "Quitting is the easiest thing to do."

12. "Inside every problem lies an opportunity."

13. "Face your fears and doubts, and new worlds will open to you."

14. "I wasn't born a natural entrepreneur. I had to be trained."

15. "Sometimes the hardest thing to do is to trust your team. It's a lesson I've had to relearn quite a few times."

16. "Success is not a stop sign."

"Most businesses think that product is the most important thing, but without great leadership, mission, and a team that delivers results at a high level, even the best product won't make a company successful." —Robert T. Kiyosaki, Entrepreneur, Author, Investor"If you are the kind of person who is waiting for the 'right' thing to happen, you might wait for a long time. It's like waiting for all the traffic lights to be green for five miles before starting the trip."

1. "Often, in the real world, it's not the smart who get ahead but the bold."

2. "The richest people in the world look for and build networks; everyone else looks for work."

3. "When times are bad is when the real entrepreneurs emerge."

4. "If you avoid failure, you also avoid success."

5. "Critics only make you stronger. You have to look at what they are saying as feedback. Sometimes the feedback helps, and other times, it's just noise that can be a distraction."

6.

7. "The thing most people don't pick up when they become an entrepreneur is that it never ends. It's 24/7."

8. "You have to look for teachers. If you want to be a mechanic, go hang out with mechanics."

9. "I believe that one key to success is to accept truth – no matter how it's spoken."

10. "Quitting is the easiest thing to do."

11. "Inside every problem lies an opportunity."

12. "Face your fears and doubts, and new worlds will open to you."

13. "I wasn't born a natural entrepreneur. I had to be trained."

14. "Sometimes the hardest thing to do is to trust your team. It's a lesson I've had to relearn quite a few times."

15. "Success is not a stop sign."

16. "Most businesses think that product is the most important thing, but without great leadership, mission, and a team that delivers results at a high level, even the best product won't make a company successful." —Robert T. Kiyosaki, Entrepreneur, Author, Investor"If you are the kind of person who is waiting for the 'right' thing to happen, you might wait for a long time. It's like waiting for all the traffic lights to be green for five miles before starting the trip."

"Often, in the real world, it's not the smart who get ahead but the bold." "The richest people in the world look for and build networks; everyone else looks for work." "When times are bad is when the real entrepreneurs emerge." "If you avoid failure, you also avoid success." "Critics only make you stronger. You have to look at what they are saying as feedback. Sometimes the feedback helps, and other times, it's just noise that can be a distraction." "The thing most people don't pick up when they become an entrepreneur is that it never ends. It's 24/7." "You have to look for teachers. If you want to be a mechanic, go hang out with mechanics." "I believe that one key to success is to accept truth – no matter how it's spoken." "Quitting is the easiest thing to do." "Inside every problem lies an opportunity." "Face your fears and doubts, and new worlds will open to you." "I wasn't born a natural entrepreneur. I had to be trained." "Sometimes the hardest thing to do is to trust your team. It's a lesson I've had to relearn quite a few times." "Success is not a stop sign." "Most businesses think that product is the most important thing, but without great leadership, mission, and a team that delivers results at a high level, even the best product won't make a company successful."

—Robert T. Kiyosaki, Entrepreneur, Author, Investor

★ Bonus: More Ways To Leverage Your Ultimate Marketing Asset

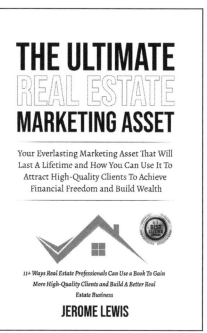

In the following section, we will uncover the transformative power a book holds for your real estate business. Having a book is not merely about adding another feather to your cap; it's a strategic move that amplifies your marketing efforts, sets you apart as an industry expert, and accelerates your business growth. This compilation of fifteen ways will reveal how your book, Your Ultimate Marketing Asset, can open up a world of opportunities. Each point highlights a unique advantage, extending from lead generation to enhancing your online presence, building trust with your audience to reducing advertising costs. As we delve into these aspects, you'll discover how your book can become an influential tool that not only expands your reach but also builds deeper relationships with your clients, ultimately fueling the success of your real estate business.

1. **Position Yourself as an Expert:** Writing a book helps you showcase your knowledge and experience, setting you apart from the competition in the real estate market.

2. **Generate Leads:** By offering your book as a free download on your website, you can attract potential clients and capture their contact details for further engagement.

3. **Impress Your Clients:** Presenting your clients with a copy of your book is a unique way of appreciating them. It's a thoughtful gift that can also lead to valuable referrals.

4. **Promote at Events:** Whether you're at a seminar, a workshop, or a meet-and-greet, your book can be sold or given away, extending your reach and enhancing your brand.

5. **Educate Your Audience:** Use your book to inform potential clients about the real estate process. This not only establishes trust but also makes them more confident in working with you.

6. **Gain Media Exposure:** A published book can attract media attention. Interviews and features can increase your visibility and promote your real estate services.

7. **Boost Your Content Marketing:** Extracts from your book can serve as valuable content for your blog or social media posts, pulling in more online traffic.

8. **Expand Your Network:** Handing over a copy of your book during networking events can leave a lasting impression and open doors for collaboration and partnerships.

9. **Enhance Your Direct Mail Campaigns:** Mailing your book to potential clients or investors makes for an impactful and personal touch.

10. **Secure Speaking Engagements:** A book to your name often translates into invitations to speak at industry events, providing you a platform to promote your expertise and services.

11. **Earn Passive Income:** Selling your book online could become an additional income stream for you.

12. **Build Trust with Your Audience:** Sharing personal experiences and case studies in your book helps to build a deeper connection with your readers, fostering trust and loyalty.

13. **Cut Advertising Costs:** Your book is a lasting promotional tool that continually delivers results, reducing the need for expensive traditional advertising.

14. **Improve Your Online Presence:** Promoting or selling your book on various online platforms can drive traffic to your website, increasing your online visibility.

15. **Grow Your Mailing List:** Offering your book in exchange for newsletter subscriptions can significantly boost your mailing list, enhancing your email marketing campaigns.

⭐Bonus: Quotes By Rich Dad, Poor Dad Author Robert Kiyosaki

Rich Dad Poor Dad Author, Robert Kiyosaki and Jerome Lewis

The Influence of Robert Kiyosaki

If there is anyone who has encapsulated the essence of financial education, entrepreneurship, and the secrets to amassing wealth through real estate, it is Robert Kiyosaki. The celebrated author of the best-selling book "Rich Dad, Poor Dad" has inspired millions across the globe with his wisdom and has had a profound influence on many, including Jerome Lewis. Kiyosaki's teachings have been instrumental in shaping Jerome's approach to the real estate industry, illuminating pathways for success and prosperity.

Wisdom from Kiyosaki's Quotes

Kiyosaki is renowned for his powerful and thought-provoking quotes that challenge conventional wisdom and inspire a new way of thinking about wealth and financial independence. Jerome has handpicked a few of these nuggets of wisdom that have resonated with him deeply and helped him navigate the vast landscape of the real estate industry. These quotes have not only shaped his understanding of the business but have also served as a guiding beacon during challenging times.

Applying Kiyosaki's Teachings in Real Estate

The following collection of quotes presents the essence of Robert Kiyosaki's teachings as perceived through the eyes of Jerome Lewis. Each quote offers unique insights into the world of real estate and exemplifies the power of financial literacy and entrepreneurship. As Jerome shares his favorite Robert Kiyosaki quotes with you, may they inspire you, motivate you, and provide you with valuable insights to thrive in your journey in the real estate industry.

Quotes:

1. "If you are the kind of person who is waiting for the 'right' thing to happen, you might wait for a long time. It's like waiting for all the traffic lights to be green for five miles before starting the trip."

2. "Often, in the real world, it's not the smart who get ahead but the bold."

3. "The richest people in the world look for and build networks; everyone else looks for work."

4. "When times are bad is when the real entrepreneurs emerge."

5. "If you avoid failure, you also avoid success."

6. "Critics only make you stronger. You have to look at what they are saying as feedback. Sometimes the feedback helps, and other times, it's just noise that can be a distraction."

7.

8. "The thing most people don't pick up when they become an entrepreneur is that it never ends. It's 24/7."

9. "You have to look for teachers. If you want to be a mechanic, go hang out with mechanics."

10. "I believe that one key to success is to accept truth – no matter how it's spoken."

11. "Quitting is the easiest thing to do."

12. "Inside every problem lies an opportunity."

13. "Face your fears and doubts, and new worlds will open to you."

14. "I wasn't born a natural entrepreneur. I had to be trained."

15. "Sometimes the hardest thing to do is to trust your team. It's a lesson I've had to relearn quite a few times."

16. "Success is not a stop sign."

17. "Most businesses think that product is the most important thing, but without great leadership, mission, and a team that delivers results at a high level, even the best product won't make a company successful." —Robert T. Kiyosaki, Entrepreneur, Author, Investor

⭐Bonus: Fraction CMO Quotes

These are the quotes throughout the book. We put them in one section for anyone that's interested.

1. "Hiring a Fractional CMO is like getting the best of both worlds - exceptional marketing expertise without the full-time financial commitment."

2. "With a Fractional CMO, you'll have someone who will inject fresh perspectives and strategies into your marketing efforts, keeping you ahead of the curve."

3. "Fractional CMOs help your business to scale - they bring big-picture thinking combined with the tactical know-how to execute strategies effectively."

4. "As a small business, hiring a Fractional CMO is like gaining a secret weapon - you get a seasoned marketing expert who is invested in your success."

5. "A Fractional CMO acts as a catalyst for growth - they can help develop and implement marketing strategies that bring results."

6. "When you hire a Fractional CMO, you're not just hiring a part-time executive, you're hiring a partner committed to the success of your marketing strategy."

7. "Fractional CMOs bring the best practices from various industries to your business, fostering innovation and creating a competitive edge."

8. "Hiring a Fractional CMO can accelerate your business growth - they're like the turbo boosts your marketing engine needs."

9. "A Fractional CMO is not just a consultant, they become an integral part of your team, focusing on results-driven marketing strategies."

10. "By hiring a Fractional CMO, you're investing in sustainable growth. They create and implement long-term strategies that benefit your business beyond their tenure."

11. "Fractional CMOs bring with them a wealth of diverse experience and insights, ready to tackle your unique business challenges head-on."

12. "The value of a Fractional CMO extends beyond the marketing department - they influence the entire business with their strategic thinking and leadership."

About The Author

"The most powerful stories are those lived, not imagined. By writing a book, you don't just tell your story, you empower others to craft their own narratives too."

 Jerome Lewis, better known as

"**Mr. Implementation**"! Jerome is

not only a **#1 National**

Best-Selling Author but also the

lead host of the highly acclaimed

Real Estate Marketing Podcast.

With over 12 books to his name, including the

best-selling "Real Estate Marketing Implementation,"

Jerome has solidified his position as a prominent figure

in the industry.

As the Chief Marketing Officer of Digital Real Estate

Strategy, an esteemed tech and marketing agency,

Jerome has assisted numerous 6-7 figure entrepreneurs

and real estate professionals in implementing,

structuring, and systematizing their tech, lead

generation, marketing implementation, and business systems.

His expertise has touched the lives of over 9854 individuals across 40 states and 4 countries.

Jerome's expertise has caught the attention of renowned companies such as Russell Brunson's ClickFunnels and Dan Kennedy's Magnetic Marketing, among others.

He has also had the privilege of sharing stages and working with some of the real estate industry's brightest minds, including Shark Tank's Kevin Harrington, Vena Jones-Cox, Krista Mashore, Matt Faircloth, and the legendary Ron LeGrand, to name just a few.

What sets Jerome apart is his unwavering commitment to getting things done, his refusal to accept excuses, and his deep passion for implementation. As a bold introvert, a dedicated father of four, and a former IT professional, Jerome brings a unique perspective to his work.

In recognition of his outstanding contributions, Jerome was honored with the prestigious Instructor of the Year Award by eXp University in 2021.

Additionally, he serves as the host of the popular weekly Real Estate Marketing Implementation & Social Media Mastermind, where he imparts his knowledge and teaches real estate professionals the intricacies of tech and marketing implementation.

Notes

THE ULTIMATE
REAL ESTATE
MARKETING ASSET

Your Everlasting Marketing Asset That Will
Last A Lifetime and How You Can Use It To
Attract High-Quality Clients To Achieve
Financial Freedom and Build Wealth

11+ Ways Real Estate Professionals Can Use a Book To Gain
More High-Quality Clients and Build A Better Real
Estate Business

JEROME LEWIS

Welcome to your personal space within this book, a haven where you can gather your thoughts, record your insights, and track your progress. This chapter is dedicated to YOU. It's an arena for your creativity, a repository for your ideas, and a sketchpad for your strategies.

As you journey through the pages of this book, each chapter will stimulate your thoughts, provoke new ideas, and ignite your inspiration. It's natural to want to capture these valuable insights, and this space is the perfect place to do just that.

You can jot down your key takeaways from each chapter, sketch out action plans, or even doodle your way to clarity. Consider this space as a dialogue between you and the book, a dialogue that extends beyond the constraints of the printed words.

Feel free to use this section as you see fit. There's no right or wrong way to take notes – it's all about what works best for you. Whether you're summarizing, mind mapping, or free-writing, it's your process that matters. It's this personal engagement with the material that will allow you to reap the most benefits from this book.

Remember, ideas are fleeting, and the thoughts you have today might be the key to your success tomorrow. So keep this chapter close, make it your companion, and let your pen flow freely. Happy noting!

Made in the USA
Columbia, SC
16 January 2024

387909d0-2c49-4b3b-b80a-e53b499eb20cR01